Rock Drumming for Beginners

How to Play Rock Drums for Beginners. Beats, Grooves and Rudiments

Rock Drumming for Beginners

How to Play Rock Drums for Beginners. Beats, Grooves and Rudiments

BY SERKAN SÜER

Published by **www.fundamental-changes.com**

ISBN 978-1-911267-60-7

www.fundamental-changes.com

Twitter: **@guitar_joseph**
Over 8000 fans on Facebook: **FundamentalChangesInGuitar**
Instagram: **FundamentalChanges**

Other Drum Books from Fundamental Changes

50 Essential Warmups for Drums

Rhythm and Notation for Drums

Other Guitar Books from Fundamental Changes

The Complete Guide to Playing Blues Guitar Book One: Rhythm Guitar

The Complete Guide to Playing Blues Guitar Book Two: Melodic Phrasing

The Complete Guide to Playing Blues Guitar Book Three: Beyond Pentatonics

The Complete Guide to Playing Blues Guitar Compilation

The CAGED System and 100 Licks for Blues Guitar

Fundamental Changes in Jazz Guitar: The Major ii V I

Minor ii V Mastery for Jazz Guitar

Jazz Blues Soloing for Guitar

Guitar Scales in Context

Guitar Chords in Context

The First 100 Chords for Guitar

Jazz Guitar Chord Mastery

Complete Technique for Modern Guitar

Funk Guitar Mastery

The Complete Technique, Theory and Scales Compilation for Guitar

Sight Reading Mastery for Guitar

Rock Guitar Un-CAGED: The CAGED System and 100 Licks for Rock Guitar

The Practical Guide to Modern Music Theory for Guitarists

Beginner's Guitar Lessons: The Essential Guide

Chord Tone Soloing for Jazz Guitar

Heavy Metal Rhythm Guitar

Heavy Metal Lead Guitar

Progressive Metal Guitar

Heavy Metal Guitar Bible

Exotic Pentatonic Soloing for Guitar

Voice Leading Jazz Guitar

The Complete Jazz Soloing Compilation

The Jazz Guitar Chords Compilation

Fingerstyle Blues Guitar

The Complete DADGAD Guitar Method

Country Guitar for Beginners

Beginner Lead Guitar Method

Contents

Introduction

The purpose of *Rock Drumming Basics* is to teach you the fundamental knowledge, skills, and ideas necessary to become an excellent rock drummer. It is designed for beginner-to-intermediate drum students with a basic knowledge of 1/4 notes and 1/8th notes. Each chapter has two main elements:

- Theoretical explanations and definitions.

- Notated and recorded examples to help you build solid and exciting rock drumming technique.

After reading and practicing the 100+ examples in this method book, you will be able to:

- Learn and internalize essential rock grooves through two-bar, and four-bar phrase examples.

- Develop your drumming technique and skill in the areas of coordination, fluency, creativity, and endurance.

- Perform with other musicians confidently.

- Develop the skills needed to self-study and improve independently of a teacher.

- Read drum notation.

I am confident that if you read and practice this book in its entirety, you will double the skills to advance your playing to a much higher level.

I wish you good luck in your drumming journey, enjoy the book!

Serkan Süer

Halifax, N.S., Canada; May 2017

Important Study Suggestions

Read everything in the book! You will probably find diving into the examples more attractive than reading carefully through each chapter before you start playing. Please read the short theory sections or you may miss important information, tips and definitions. To get the most out of your practice time I strongly recommend that you read the book in its entirety.

Use a metronome. Practicing with a metronome will help you develop your skills more quickly. The initial tempo for each example is 50 beats per minute (bpm). Once an exercise is comfortable and accurate you should increase your speed gradually and incrementally.

Practice regularly. Practicing exercises everyday (at least 45 minutes) will quickly increase your overall development. If you can't create time everyday, try to practice at least twice a week.

Repeat the examples again and again. When training, repetition is very important. Play each exercise in different tempos to improve your skills and establish *muscle memory*. Practice each groove example repeatedly while using different ride pattern surfaces (closed hi-hats, open hi-hats, ride cymbal, floor tom, cowbell, etc.), and different snare drum options (cross-stick, or rim-shot beats).

Listen to the audio while practicing. Hearing the audio will help you learn the examples more easily.

Create your own exercises. After finishing each chapter, get creative and write your own variations. This will help you 'get inside' drumming, and develop a much deeper understanding of the music.

Practice each bar individually before learning the full example. As you will see, the examples for this book are written in two-bar or four-bar phrases. These phrases will help you understand the logic of grooves better. However, you should also practice each bar individually to focus on specific technical improvements.

Play the opposite hand combinations: Start each example with your weaker hand. Hand combinations are given for some examples in the book. If you are a left-handed drummer, or if you are right-handed drummer, and you want to develop your technique, practice the examples with the opposite leading hand combinations.

Learn from legendary drummers.

Check out: Buddy Rich, Bernard Purdie, John Bonham, Ian Paice, Ringo Starr, John Densmore, Ronnie Wood, Mitch Mitchell, Cozy Powell, Jeff Porcaro, Phil Collins, Simon Philips, Neil Peart, Steve Smith, Tico Torres, Steven Adler, Dave Weckl, Steve Gadd, Jim Payne, Yoron Israel, Dennis Chambers, Omar Hakim, Rod Morgenstein, Mike Mangini, Mike Portnoy, Vinnie Colaiuta, Thomas Lang, Gavin Harrison, Virgil Donati, Matt Cameron, Chad Smith, Dave Grohl, Chris Adler, Lars Ulrich, Nicko McBrain, Nick Menza, Jimmy DeGrasso, Dave Lombardo, Joy Jordison, Marco Minnemann, Derek Roddy and many others… Listen to different eras, styles, bands, songs, techniques and different musical approaches.

Listening to, and learning from legendary drummers will have a positive effect on your drumming skills and your musicality.

The notation used in this book is as follows:

Notation Key

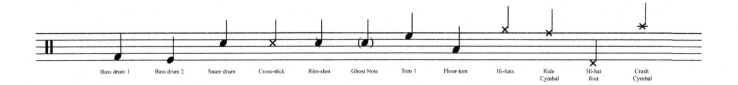

Get the Audio

The audio files for this book are available to download for free from **www.fundamental-changes.com** and the link is in the top right corner. Simply select this book title from the drop-down menu and follow the instructions to get the audio.

We recommend that you download the files directly to your computer, not to your tablet, and extract them there before adding them to your media library. You can then put them on your tablet, iPod or burn them to CD.

On the download page there is a help PDF and we also provide technical support via the contact form.

Kindle / eReaders

To get the most out of this book, remember that you can double tap any image to enlarge it. Turn off 'column viewing' and hold your Kindle in landscape mode.

Twitter: @guitar_joseph
FB: FundamentalChangesInGuitar
Instagram: FundamentalChanges

Chapter One

1/4-Note Ride Patterns and 1/8th-Note Fills

A *ride pattern* is a steady and rhythmic section of a bar or a phrase that is played on one surface (such as hi-hats, open hi-hats, ride cymbal, ride bell, floor tom, cowbell, etc.), and gives the groove its continuous feel. Any part of a drum-kit can be used as a ride pattern surface.

If a ride pattern is created with 1/4-note beats, it is called a *1/4-note ride pattern*. Practicing 1/4-note ride patterns in 4/4 time signatures is a great starting point for building rhythmic knowledge and drumming technique.

We will now study ride patterns and begin to develop hand-to-foot coordination too. This coordination is essential to master to become a good drummer.

Here is a simple rock groove with a 1/4-note ride pattern. Count and play the 1/4-note ride pattern on closed hi-hats.

Example 1a:

Playing on different ride pattern surfaces is an effective way to enhance the grooves.

Play the 1/4-note ride pattern on ride cymbal in bars one and two, and on open hi-hats in bars three and four.

Example 1b:

Another way to enhance the groove is to change the snare drum technique. If you lay your stick flat on the snare drum and hit it on the rim, you will create a *cross-stick beat*. Cross-stick beats have a sharp 'click' sound and are usually played during the softer parts of rock songs.

If you hit the snare drum's skin and its rim at the same time, you will create a *rim-shot beat.* Rim-shots have a deeper and stronger sound. They are usually played during the louder parts of rock songs. Practice these two snare drum techniques with the previous rock grooves.

Now play the 1/4-note ride pattern on closed hi-hats and play the snare drum beats as cross-stick beats.

Example 1c:

In the following example, Play the 1/4-note ride pattern on closed hi-hats and play rim-shots on the snare drum…

Example 1d:

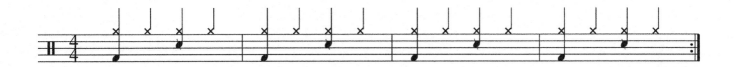

The following examples show some simple bass drum and snare drum variations. Focus on accuracy and make sure that your feet and hands synchronise perfectly.

Example 1e:

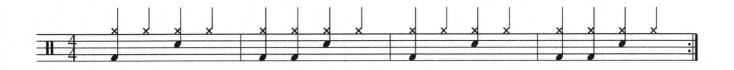

Example 1f:

Example 1g:

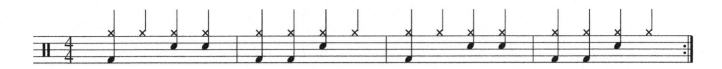

Example 1h:

1/8th-Note Bass and Snare Drum Variations

1/4 notes are divided into two equal divisions to create 1/8th notes. Using 1/4 notes and 1/8th notes together in the same grooves is a creative idea for technical development. You can choose to play the 1/8th notes on the bass drum or snare drum to create more colourful grooves.

Begin by combining 1/8th-note bass drum beats with 1/4-note ride patterns to build your bass drum technique:

Example 1i:

Example 1j:

Now, practice combining 1/8th-note snare beats with a 1/4-note ride patterns. The following examples will help you develop better two-hand coordination:

Example 1k:

Example 1l:

1/8th-Note Rudiments: Single-stroke, and Double-stroke Rolls

Rudiments are the foundation of all drumming and are played with specific sticking combinations. You should practice them on the snare drum before moving them to the entire drum-kit to develop your sticking skills, reflexes, endurance and creativity.

It is easy to create grooves and fills based on rudiments, and they are a drummer's essential tools for musical development. Before practicing some simple 1/8th-note rudiments, let's check out how to count 1/8th-notes in a 4/4-time signature. Play the following example on the snare and count out loud. Accent the first beat in every bar with your voice.

Example 1m:

The following examples show the 1/8th-note single-stroke roll and double-stroke roll rudiments. Pay careful attention to the sticking written underneath the notation. It is *vital* to go slowly and ensure you are playing each exercise correctly.

1/8th-note single-stroke roll.

Example 1n:

1/8th-note double-stroke roll.

Example 1o:

Example 1p: In the next example, a 1/4-note foot pattern is played with the hi-hat foot and bass drum. Play along using both 1/8th-note rudiments with this pattern to improve your coordination.

Play the following example with both a single-note, and a double-note roll.

Groove Variations with 1/8th-Note Fills

Adding a *fill* at the end of a rhythmic phrase is an important structure in rock drumming. The following examples will help you to learn this structure and prepare you for more complex rock grooves later. Each example has a four-bar phrase groove variation with 1/8th-note fill in the final bar. You will have heard this structure many times in pop, rock, blues and jazz music.

Pay attention to the sticking throughout each fill, and notice whether a single-stroke or double-stroke roll is used.

Example 1q:

Example 1r:

Example 1s:

Example 1t:

That's all for Chapter One. You have started to discover the basic skills of rock drumming so practice each exercise carefully with a metronome. Start with the click set to 50bpm. This is your 1/4-note pulse. When you can play an example through *three times perfectly*, raise the tempo 5bpm and stay at that speed until you can again play it perfectly three times. Incrementally increase the speed up to about 120 bpm.

However, don't stay on just one exercise and get it up to 120bpm before moving to the next. Make time to practice all the exercises in this chapter each day, and keep a diary of your progress. This means that you can start each new practice session picking up where you left off. Of course, after 24 hours rest, you may have to drop the metronome speed a little while you familiarise yourself with each exercise again.

Chapter Two

1/8th-Note Ride Patterns and Fills

In this chapter, you will continue to develop your primary drumming skills by learning some essential 1/8th-note ride patterns. 1/8th-note ride patterns are fundamental in rock drumming and are usually practiced over *backbeats*.

A backbeat is formed by a characteristic sharp snare accent on beats 2 and 4 of a bar. Beats 1 and 3 are played by the bass drum.

The following are common rock groove variations with 1/8th note ride pattern and backbeats:

Count and play the following 1/8th-note ride pattern on closed hi-hats.

Example 2a:

Now play the pattern on the ride cymbal.

(Also try adding 1/4-note hi-hat foot beats to develop your coordination and balance. The hi-hat foot beats are notated in bars three and bar four).

Example 2b:

Play the next ride pattern on closed hi-hats and play the snare drum with a cross-stick.

Example 2c:

Play the following 1/8th-note ride pattern on closed hi-hats with as rim-shots on the snare.

Example 2d:

These fundamental grooves are the most important to learn, and many great rock songs are created with very simple grooves, like the ones shown above.

For example, Little Richard's Long Tall Sally, Tom Petty and The Heartbreakers' I Won't Back Down, The Steve Miller Band's The Joker, AC DC's Thunderstruck, T.N.T. and Highway to Hell all emphasise the importance of the getting the basics right.

The simplest way to create different rock grooves is to use different 1/8th-note bass drum variations. Check out the following examples:

Example 2e:

Example 2f:

Example 2g:

The following example shows a *Four-on-the-floor* bass drum pattern.

Example 2h:

You can hear similar bass drum variations to the above few examples in Coldplay's Yellow, Lenny Kravitz's Again, and Scorpion's Wind of Change. Queen's Another One Bites the Dust has a four on the floor bass drum pattern.

Backbeat Variations:

Another creative way to enhance 1/8th-note ride pattern grooves is to use backbeat variations. These are like bass drum variations, but the backbeat (usually snare) is varied on beats 2 and 4.

Double backbeats are a popular addition and are generally used in Rock and Roll grooves.

Example 2i: Double backbeats.

The Beatles', I Wanna Hold Your Hand, and Pearl Jam's cover of Last Kiss have double backbeats in their grooves. (Last Kiss was originally released by Wayne Cochran).

The following examples show other backbeat variations. Each variation has a specific name and they are played in many different rock genres. Practice them carefully:

Single backbeat.

Example 2j:

Half-time feel.

Example 2k:

Double-time feel.

Example 2l:

Replaced backbeats.

Example 2m:

'Straight four' snare drum pattern.

Example 2n:

Playing toms as backbeats.

Example 2o:

Accented Notes

Accents are notes that are played intentionally stronger. These notes are indicated by an accent mark (>).

Playing accented notes on 1/8th-note ride patterns is a useful technique that adds interest to the groove. While practicing this technique, pay attention to the difference in sound between the accented notes and the others. Use your lower arm and wrist more, and hit with the shank of the stick to play distinguishable accented notes.

In the following example, play the accents with the hi-hat on each 1/4 note beat. This pattern is often used in hard rock, grunge, and metal grooves.

Example 2p:

Now play the accents on the second 1/8th note of each beat. This pattern is commonly used in funk-rock, and alternative/pop-rock grooves.

Example 2q:

Open/Closed Hi-Hat Beats

Playing open (o) and closed (+) hi-hat beats is an effective technique that creates a different sound and feel in any groove. It directly changes the *melody* of the groove.

Play any ride pattern on the closed hi-hats. Release the hi-hat foot to create the open hi-hat sound when desired. Step on the pedal again to close the hi-hats. Your foot movements must be sharp for this technique to work.

The following examples will quickly develop your technique:

Example 2r:

Example 2s:

Listen to The Rolling Stones' Anybody Seen My Baby. This song has a cool groove that cleverly uses open and closed hi-hat beats.

1/8th-Note Rudiment: Single Paradiddle

The 1/8th-note single paradiddle is a vital rudiment to develop your sticking and drumming skills. It is a combination of single-stroke roll and double-stroke roll rudiments. Practice the important examples below:

1/8th-note single paradiddle.

Example 2t:

The following 1/4-note foot pattern is created with hi-hat foot and bass drum beats. Combine it with a 1/8th-note single paradiddle rudiment on the snare.

Example 2u:

Groove Variations with 1/8th-Note Fills

In the previous chapter, you practiced combining 1/8th-note fills with 1/4-note ride pattern grooves.

Now it's time to practice 1/8th-note fills with 1/8th-note ride patterns in four-bar phrases to develop more complex rock beats. Pay attention to the sticking hand combinations given for the fills in bar four.

Example 2v:

Example 2w:

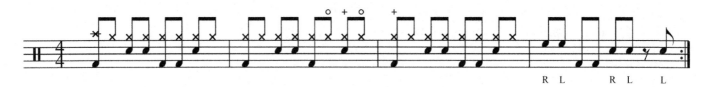

Example 2x:

Example 2y:

In the next example, play the accented notes on the ride bell and the unaccented notes on the ride cymbal surface. This is a common ride cymbal pattern.

Example 2z:

The exercises in this chapter are the start of an exciting journey into one of the most fundamental aspects of rock drumming. Come up with your own examples and remember to practice incrementally with a metronome. In the next chapter, we will study how to make grooves with 1/16th-note rhythms.

Chapter Three

1/16th-Note Ride Patterns and 1/16th-Note Fills

When you have mastered 1/4-note and 1/8th-note ride patterns, you are ready to learn another commonly used approach, 1/16th-note ride patterns.

1/16th note ride patterns can either be played with one hand, or two hands. It is essential to develop both techniques to improve your drum skills.

Let's take a closer look at these important techniques:

One Hand 1/16th-Note Ride Patterns

As more notes are played in 1/16th-note ride patterns they can be more difficult to play. At slow to medium tempos, drummers generally prefer to play 1/16th-note ride patterns with one hand.

Count and practice the following examples attentively.

The first example shows the counting of 1/16th-notes. Play the 1/16th-note ride pattern on closed hi-hats with one hand.

Example 3a*:*

Example 3b:

Example 3c:

Half-time feel.

Example 3d:

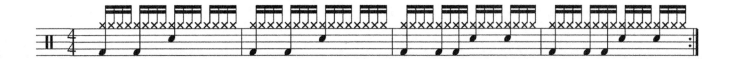

Double-time feel.

Example 3e:

Alice in Chains' Down in a Hole has a colourful groove that uses 1/16th-note ride patterns. The tempo is manageable so the ride pattern is played with one hand. You can hear many different groove variations in the same song.

One Hand 1/16th-Note Ride Pattern Variations

Now let's practice playing some ride pattern variations with one hand. As before, pay attention to the counting of each variation.

Listen to Eric Clapton's Wonderful Tonight and The Eagles' Hotel California to hear different uses of this first variation.

Example 3f:

The following variations are all commonly used and will help to develop your technique. Go slow and use a metronome.

Example 3g:

Example 3h:

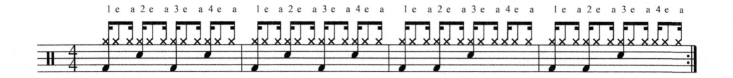

Two Hand 1/16th-Note Ride Patterns

Playing 1/16th-note ride patterns with two hands is a significant drumming technique. The two-hand sticking combination is called the *alternating hands technique*. The hand combination is 'R L R L…' or 'L R L R…' This technique is generally used on closed, or open hi-hats in rock at higher tempos.

Any 1/16th-note ride pattern played with one hand can also be played using the alternating hands technique.

To begin, play this 1/16th-note pattern on closed hi-hats with two hands.

Example 3i:

Work through the following ideas to get a feel for 1/16th note, alternating hands technique.

Example 3j:

Example 3k:

Half-time feel.

Example 3l:

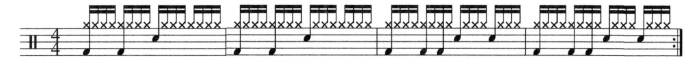

Double-time feel.

Example 3m:

Check out Deep Purple's Smoke on the Water to hear how the alternating hands technique is used in the classic rock genre. The ride patterns are played during the intro and the melody sections of the song. Also listen to Red Hot Chilli Peppers' *Parallel Universe* as a great example of alternating hands in modern alternative/funk rock genre.

The alternating hand technique is not the only option for playing with two hands. You can also develop various hand combinations and rudiments as your skills improve.

Two-Hand Ride Variations with Combinations

Two-hand combination 1/16th-note ride pattern variations are not as complicated as they look. If you pay attention to the hand combinations and have patience, you can improve your technique easily.

These combinations help you to play at faster tempos and create stronger beats. However, you should practice at slower tempos first before speeding up gradually. Each of following examples offers you two different combinations.

Alternative two-handed combination: *R LLR LLR LLR LL.*

Example 3n:

Alternative two-handed combination: *RLL RLL RLL RLL.*

Example 3o:

Alternative two-handed combination: *RL RLR L RL RLR L.*

Example 3p:

1/16th-Note Rudiments: Single-stroke Roll, Double-stroke Roll and Single Paradiddle

We have covered 1/8th-note single-stroke roll, double-stroke roll, and single paradiddle rudiments in the previous chapters. Now, we will focus on the 1/16th-note versions of the same rudiments. The following examples will help you develop your coordination and sticking technique.

The first example shows the 1/16th-note single-stroke roll.

Example 3q:

RLRLRLRLRLRLRLRL   RLRLRLRLRLRLRLRL   RLRLRLRLRLRLRLRL   RLRLRLRLRLRLRLRL

Here is the 1/16th-note double-stroke roll.

Example 3r:

RRLLRRLLRRLLRRLL   RRLLRRLLRRLLRRLL   RRLLRRLLRRLLRRLL   RRLLRRLLRRLLRRLL

1/16th-note single paradiddle.

Example 3s:

RLRRLRLLRLRRLRLL   RLRRLRLLRLRRLRLL   RLRRLRLLRLRRLRLL   RLRRLRLLRLRRLRLL

Play each rudiment with a 1/4-note hi-hat foot pattern as shown in bar one and bar two. Then play each rudiment with the 1/8th-note hi-hat foot pattern as shown in bar three and bar four. Listen to the audio to hear this in action.

Example 3t:

Groove Variations with 1/16th-Note Fills

1/16th-note fills are used in various genres and are based on 1/16th-note rudiments and hand combinations.

Practice the following groove examples carefully; these examples will help you to develop 1/16th-note fill ideas and will prepare you to play more complex grooves later.

Each of following examples contains two fills. Play them in bars two and four of each phrase:

The first example combines an 1/8th-note ride pattern with 1/16th-note fills.

Example 3u:

Example 3v:

Example 3w:

The next example is built around a 1/16th-note ride pattern (alternating hands) with two 1/16th-note fills.

Example 3x:

Play this 1/16th-note ride pattern variation (sticking with one hand) and add the 1/16th-note fills.

Example 3y:

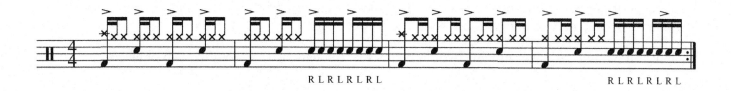

As 1/16th-note rhythms contain more notes, their rhythmic permutations are almost unlimited. Get creative in your practice and see how many ideas you can come up with. Explore single- and alternate-hand sticking.

Chapter Four

1/8th-Note Groove Variations and Ghost Notes

After studying different ride patterns in the previous three chapters, we will now focus on creating and playing more colourful and complex groove variations. The most common way to enhance rock grooves is to combine 1/16th-note bass drum beats with 1/8th-note ride patterns.

Through the following examples, you will learn how to use 1/16th-note syncopated (off-beat) bass drum beats while improving your drum technique. Count out loud as this will help you to play in time and internalise the rhythms.

Example 4a:

Example 4b:

Example 4c:

You can hear similar syncopated bass drum variations in Pink Floyd's Comfortably Numb, Led Zeppelin's Kashmir, and Coldplay's In My Place.

Playing open/closed hi-hat beats with syncopated bass drum beats in the same groove is another way to create colourful and funky variations:

Example 4d:

Example 4e:

Example 4f:

An effective way to create different grooves is by playing 1/16th-note syncopated snare drum beats with 1/8th-note ride patterns:

Example 4g:

Example 4h:

Example 4i:

You can hear similar snare drum variations in Bush's Machinehead and Stiltskin's Inside.

Ghost Notes on the Snare Drum

Ghost notes are played much softer and quieter than others; they add to a phrase's 'depth', creating a percussive effect and a groovier feel. They are shown as normal notes in parentheses ( ) and can be played on any part of the kit. They are, however, particularly common on the snare drums.

It is common to hear ghost notes in all styles of music and they are common in jazz, Latin, funk, soul, and pop, etc. Practicing ghost notes in grooves will improve your sensitivity and help you to develop the basis of other styles.

Check out the ghost notes in the grooves below.

Example 4j:

Example 4k:

Example 4l:

Example 4m:

One creative idea to play open and closed hi-hat with ghost notes together to create an interesting groove.

Example 4n:

You can also combine 1/16th-note ride variations with open/closed hi-hats backbeats, and ghost notes together in the same groove. The following is a challenging example to end the chapter.

Example 4o:

Check out The Red Hot Chili Peppers' Californication, Scar Tissue, and Otherside, and you will hear many different ghost note variations.

Chapter Five

1/8th-Note Triplet and Shuffle Patterns

1/8th-note triplet, and shuffle ride patterns are common grooves in rock. They have a different feel than the patterns you have learned so far.

1/8th-Note Triplet Ride Patterns

When 1/4 notes are divided into three equal beats we create 1/8th-note triplets (three notes per beat). Ride patterns based around these rhythms are unsurprisingly called *1/8th-note triplet ride patterns*. The next two examples show how this groove works.

First, here's how to count 1/8th-note triplets. Play this pattern on closed hi-hats.

Example 5a:

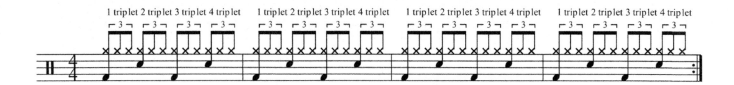

Now play the 1/8th-note triplet pattern on the ride cymbal. Add 1/4-note hi-hat foot beats to the groove in bars three and four to test your coordination.

Example 5b:

Bass and snare drum variations can be used to create different grooves with 1/8th-note triplet ride patterns:

Example 5c:

Example 5d:

Example 5e:

Half-time feel.

Example 5f:

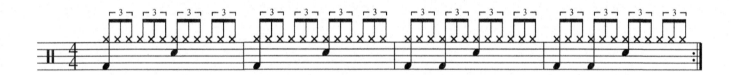

The next example has a double-time feel.

Example 5g:

Bon Jovi's Bed of Roses, Queen's We are the Champions, and R.E.M.'s Everybody Hurts have 1/8th-note triplet ride pattern grooves.

Listening to these songs will help you better understand triplet ride patterns.

1/8th-Note Shuffle Ride Patterns

The 1/8th-note shuffle is a rhythmic formation that consists of 1/8th-note triplets with the middle notes missing.

These can be tricky to feel at first. Try setting your metronome to around 150 bpm and hearing each click as a triplet 1/8th note. This means that three clicks are one beat. You can then play the first and third click while missing out the middle one.

Count out loud,

"Trip – er – let Trip – er – let Trip – er – let Trip – er – let".

with one syllable per click.

Next, replace the word 'trip' with the beat count, so now say,

"ONE – er – let Two – er – let three – er – let Four – er – let".

Finally, miss out the middle syllable, "er"

"One – Let Two – Let Three – Let Four – let".

Listen carefully to the audio before playing the following examples.

Here's the counting of 1/8th-note shuffle pattern. Play it on closed hi-hats.

Example 5h:

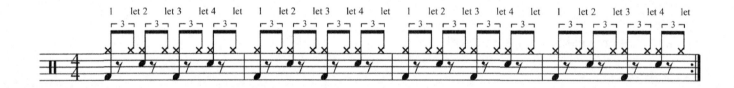

Now play the pattern on the ride cymbal.

Example 5i:

You can use bass and snare drum variations to enhance 1/8th-note shuffle ride patterns. Make sure you keep the shuffle feel while practicing the following examples.

Example 5j:

Example 5k:

Example 5l:

Queen's Crazy Little Thing Called Love, Tragically Hip's Courage, and Muse's Uprising are great examples of shuffle rock.

This half-time shuffle is a challenging variation.

Example 5m:

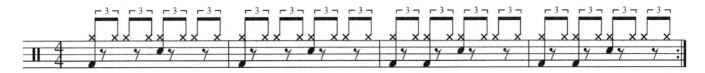

Now add some ghost notes to the half-time shuffle ride pattern. Toto's Rosanna has an awesome half-time shuffle groove with ghost notes.

Example 5n:

Here's a double-time shuffle.

Example 5o:

Swing is the fundamental rhythm of jazz. It is created from a combination of 1/4 notes and 1/8th-note shuffle.

Example 5p: Swing-feel.

You can hear shuffle and swing-feel grooves in classic rock 'n' roll songs. Elvis Presley's Blue Suede Shoes and Hound Dog, and The Everly Brothers' Bye Bye Love are good examples.

1/8th-Note Triplet Rudiments: Single-stroke Roll and Double Paradiddle

The 1/8th-note triplet single-stroke roll and double paradiddle are the rudiments you will learn in this chapter. By practicing the following exercises, you will develop sticking technique and coordination.

Begin with the 1/8th-note triplet single-stroke roll.

Example 5q:

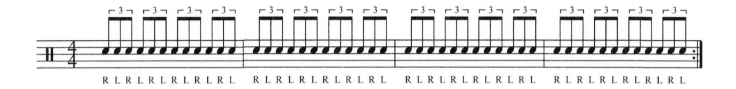

Now try the 1/8th-note triplet double paradiddle. Be careful with the sticking!

Example 5r:

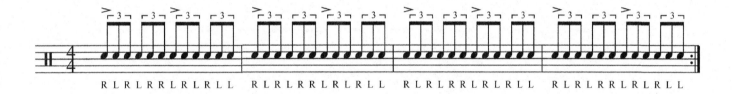

Play each rudiment with a 1/4-note bass drum pattern in bars one and two, then with a 1/4-note hi-hat foot pattern in bars three and four.

Example 5s:

Groove Variations with 1/8th-Note Triplet Fills

Triplet and shuffle rhythms can be played together in phrases and fills. 1/8th-note fills can be played with both 1/8th-note triplet ride patterns and 1/8th-note shuffle ride patterns.

The following variations are based on these concepts and will help you to develop 1/8th-note triplet fill ideas while preparing you for more complex 1/8th-note triplet grooves.

Each of the following examples contains two, one-bar fills. Play the triplet fills in bars two and four of each phrase and pay careful attention to the sticking.

Example 5t:

Example 5u:

Example 5v:

Example 5w:

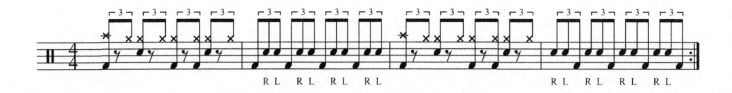

Example 5x:

Chapter Six

Back to the Roots: Blues Drumming

The Blues is at the root of all rock drumming. It is fundamental not only for rock, but also for jazz, funk, R&B, rap, and many more styles. Since the early 1900s, blues music has influenced the development of every modern music genre, so learning blues drumming is a necessity for every drummer.

1/16th-Note Sextuplet Rudiment: Single-stroke Roll

1/16th-note sextuplets are used in many blues grooves, so it is important to understand them before launching into the rest of the chapter. 1/16th-note sextuplets are created when 1/4 note rhythms are divided into six equal divisions.

Practice the examples below to improve your sticking technique and coordination. Listen to the audio before playing the following examples because 1/16th note sextuplets can be difficult to grasp at first.

Here is the counting of 1/16th-note sextuplets. Count them aloud before and as you play them.

Example 6a:

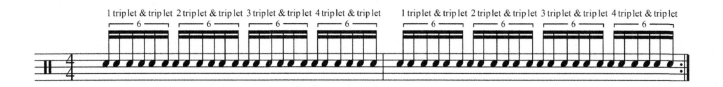

Try this 1/16th-note sextuplet single-stroke roll.

Example 6b:

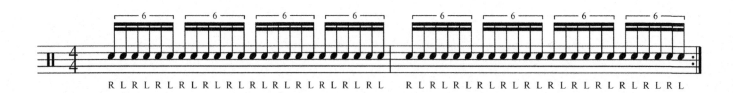

Now add a 1/4-note foot pattern.

Example 6c:

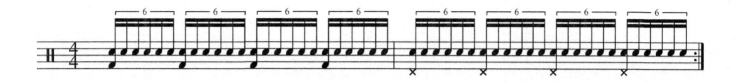

The preliminary exercises above will stand you in good stead for the rest of this chapter and help you to develop more control and technique in your playing.

Slow Blues

The slow blues style is all based on 1/8th-note triplet ride patterns.

Begin by playing this pattern on closed hi-hats.

Example 6d:

The slow blues beat is often written in a 12/8 time signature because it naturally divides into four groups of three (4x3 = 12). This gives four beats with three subdivisions and saves writing all the triplets above the notes as shown above. The 4/4 example above is written below in 12/8 and the two examples sound identical.

Example 6e:

Now play the 1/8th-note triplet ride pattern on the ride cymbal. Play hi-hat foot notes on the 2nd and 4th beats of each bar.

Example 6f:

Next try playing the 1/8th-note triplet pattern on closed hi-hats.

Example 6g:

Let's "double up" and add a 1/16th note sextuplet on the second triplet of beats 1 and 3.

Example 6h:

Now play an 1/8th-note triplet fill in bar two and a1/16th-note fill in bar four.

Example 6i:

Ray Charles' Night Time Is the Right Time is a great example of drumming in the slow blues genre. Also, listen to Gary Moore's Still Got the Blues. This blues rock-style song has a characteristic groove.

Medium and Up-Tempo Shuffles

Other important blues styles include the *medium tempo shuffle (90 – 140 bpm)*, and *the up-tempo shuffle (160bpm+)*. The following four-bar variations can be played in both tempo ranges.

Play the following shuffle ride patterns on the ride cymbal and place hi-hat footnotes on the 2nd and 4th 1/4 beats of each bar:

Example 6j:

Example 6k:

Example 6l:

Check out B.B. King's Rock Me Baby as an example of medium tempo shuffle blues. You can also listen to John Lee Hooker's Boom Boom Boom to hear an up-tempo shuffle blues.

The Traditional Chicago-style Shuffle

The Chicago Shuffle has a unique shuffle pattern, which is also known as the *double shuffle* groove. The ride cymbal and snare are dominant in this groove, with both being played together throughout.

Example 6m:

The Twelve-Bar Blues

The most common blues form is the *twelve-bar blues*. A "twelve-bar" is a blues form that has a specific harmonic (chord) structure and is twelve bars long. In its most simple form, the twelve-bar blues is based on the I, IV and V chords of a key. For example, in the key of E, these chords would be E Major, A Major and B Major.

Drummers follow and outline the twelve-bar formation and keep the blues groove moving forward. At the end of bar twelve, the whole structure repeats.

The following example shows a twelve-bar blues medium tempo shuffle pattern.

The first time through, play the 1/8th-note shuffle ride pattern on closed hi-hats. On the repeat, play the pattern on the ride cymbal:

Example 6n:

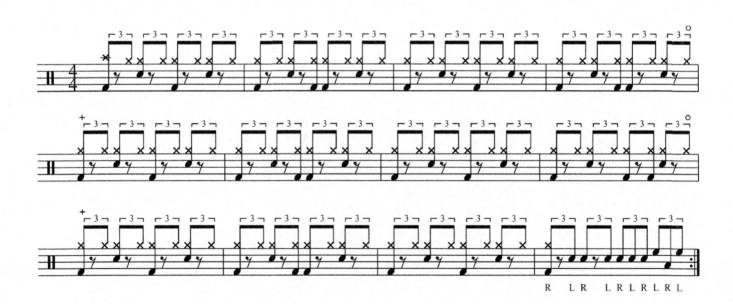

The Blues Brothers' version of Sweet Home Chicago is a perfect example of a twelve-bar, medium tempo shuffle blues, and was first recorded by guitarist Robert Johnson.

We have covered some blues styles that are based on 1/8th-note triplet, and shuffle rhythms. However, there are also many blues songs based on straight 1/8th-note rock beats.

Jimi Hendrix, Steve Ray Vaughan, Garry Moore, Eric Clapton, and many more artists/bands have all merged straight rock beats with the blues to form "blues rock".

Chapter Seven

Developing Technique: More Essential Rudiments

I mentioned at the beginning of the previous chapter that practicing rudiments is the best way for drummers to improve their technique and rhythm.

This chapter is designed to help you develop various important rudiments and stick control exercises. By practicing these examples, you will be able to develop your creativity, flexibility, endurance, coordination, and technique.

1/16th-Note Rolls

1/16th-note rolls are created by combining double-stroke rolls with one accented single-stroke. For example, the five-stroke roll contains two doubles and one single-stroke.

The following examples demonstrate 1/16th-note five, seven, nine, eleven, thirteen and fifteen stroke rolls.

Example 7a: 1/16th-note five stroke roll.

Example 7b: 1/16th-note seven stroke roll.

Example 7c: 1/16th-note nine stroke roll.

Example 7d: 1/16th-note eleven stroke roll.

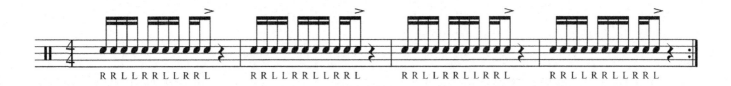

Example 7e: 1/16th-note thirteen stroke roll.

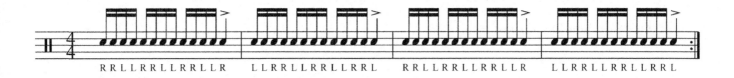

Example 7f: 1/16th-note fifteen stroke roll.

Practice these rolls incrementally with a metronome, and when you start to get comfortable on the snare (or practice pad), play on other surfaces before moving them round the kit to create your own fills.

Flams

A *flam* is comprised of two single-strokes that are played from different stick heights and with different strengths. Because the sticks start from different heights but move with the same speed to the drum head, this creates a fractional gap between the two contacts.

The first stroke is called the *grace note*. The grace note is played softly from a low height and doesn't have any rhythmic value. The second stroke is called the *primary note*. The primary is played stronger with the stick starting at a higher height. The grace note is played fractionally before the primary note to produce a thicker and longer combined sound.

The grace note must be struck very slightly before the primary and is always played with the opposite hand. Normally, only the sticking direction for the primary note will be given. You can see the notation below. If more than one grace note is played before the primary, this is called a *drag*.

Check out these flam-based rudiments.

1/4-note flams, variation one.

Example 7g:

1/4-note flams, variation two.

Example 7h:

Try these 1/8th-note flams based on the single-stroke roll.

Example 7i:

This 1/8th-note 'flam tab' is based on the double-stroke roll.

Example 7j:

RRLLRRLL RRLLRRLL RRLLRRLL RRLLRRLL

Here's an 1/8th-note 'flam paradiddle' based on the single-stroke roll.

Example 7k:

RLRRLRLL RLRRLRLL RLRRLRLL RLRRLRLL

We can also flam in triplets. Check out these 1/8th-note triplet flams.

Example 7l:

RLRLRLRLRLRL RLRLRLRLRLRL RLRLRLRLRLRL RLRLRLRLRLRL

A *drag* is a flam with more than one grace note. Here are some 1/4-note drags.

Example 7m:

R L R L R L R L R L R L R L R L

As before, work with a metronome to increase your speed, technique and confidence before moving these ideas around the kit to create your own fills.

1/16th-Note Sextuplet Rudiments

The following rudiments are essential. In this section, you will learn how to play 1/16th-note sextuplet double-stroke rolls, double paradiddles and paradiddle-diddle rudiments.

Example 7n: 1/16th-note sextuplet double-stroke roll.

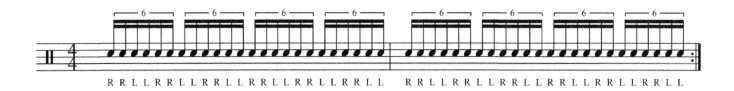

Example 7o: 1/16th-note sextuplet double paradiddle.

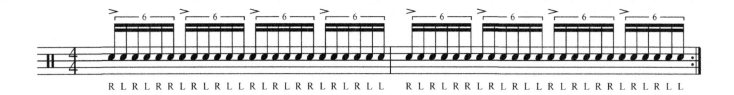

Example 7p: 1/16th-note sextuplet paradiddle-diddle.

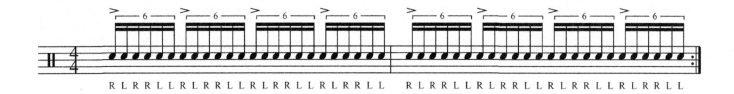

1/32nd-Notes Rudiments

Straight 1/16th notes are divided into two equal divisions to create 1/32nd notes. The 1/32nd-note single-stroke roll and double-stroke roll rudiments are shown in the following examples:

Example 7r: 1/32nd-note single-stroke roll.

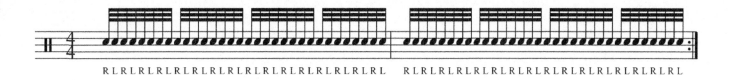

RLRLRLRLRLRLRLRLRLRLRLRLRLRLRLRL   RLRLRLRLRLRLRLRLRLRLRLRLRLRLRLRL

Example 7s: 1/32nd-note double-stroke roll.

RRLLRRLLRRLLRRLLRRLLRRLLRRLLRRLL   RRLLRRLLRRLLRRLLRRLLRRLLRRLLRRLL

Don't worry too much about 1/32nd notes for now. Spend more time on 1/16th- and 1/8th-note rhythms as these are your bread and butter as a modern drummer.

'Alternating Hand' Combinations

Now let's develop your alternating hand techniques (R L R L… or L R L R…) in different combinations so that you can build control over the kit.

The following examples will teach you to combine odd and even note divisions together in the same bar. This will make you focus in detail on your rhythm. These ideas can be used to create very interesting fills although you must practice them very carefully because combing odd and even note groupings is very challenging.

Record your practice sessions when working on these ideas and always work with a metronome. You will quickly hear where you start to speed up and slow down through the exercises.

Let's start by combining 1/8th notes and 1/8th-note triplets. It is common to speed up too much when moving into triplets and slow down too much when moving back to straight 1/8ths. Pay attention to the metronome.

Example 7t:

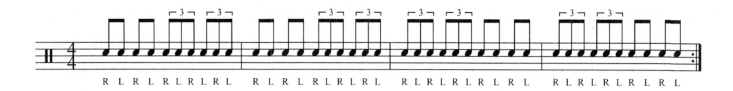

This next exercise is difficult. Combine 1/8th-note triplets and 1/16th notes together. Set the metronome to about 60bpm and record your playing.

Example 7u:

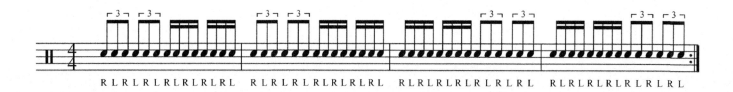

In the following exercise, you will learn to switch between 1/8th-note triplets and 1/16th-note triplets. Think about 'double-timing' the 1/8ths to create 1/16ths

Example 7v:

RLRLRLRLRLRLRLRLRL RLRLRLRLRLRLRLRLRLRL RLRLRLRLRLRLRLRLRLRLRL RLRLRLRLRLRLRLRLRLRL

Now work on different 1/16th-note variations together. Dotted notes are written in bar one and bar two. The dot increases the note's value by half of its original value.

In this example, the dot increases the value of the 1/8th notes by a 1/16th note so it lasts for 3 1/16th notes.

Example 7w:

RLRLRL RLRLR L   RLRLRL RLRLR L   RLRL RLR LRLRLRL   RLRL RLR LRLRLRL

Chapter Eight

Dynamics

Dynamics tell musicians how loud or soft to play. They make the music come alive and add an important extra dimension. Dynamics are shown by their *Italian* names, and abbreviated so they are easily recognised by musicians.

The most commonly used dynamics are shown below.

Symbol	Term	Effect
pp	*Pianissimo*	*Very soft*
p	*Piano*	*Soft*
mp	*Mezzo Piano*	*Medium soft*
mf	*Mezzo Forte*	*Medium loud*
f	*Forte*	*Loud*
ff	*Fortissimo*	*Very loud*

Piano, mezzo forte, and forte are the three dynamic levels that you will study in this chapter. These are the ones commonly used in rock.

Piano refers to playing soft and quietly. Check out the following examples and be sure to stay in control of your dynamics throughout the exercises.

Example 8a:

Example 8b:

Example 8c:

Example 8d:

Mezzo forte refers to playing at a medium volume and with medium strength. Mezzo forte is what is commonly defined as a "normal" playing volume

Play through the following examples with the correct sticking, and concentrate on controlling the volume of every note.

Example 8e:

Example 8f:

Example 8g:

Example 8h:

Forte refers to playing stronger and louder. Play the following examples loudly:

Example 8i:

Example 8j:

Example 8k:

Example 8l:

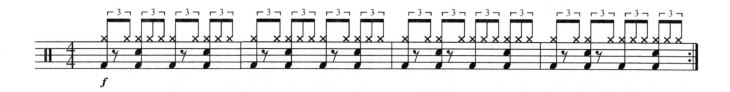

Now you have worked on each dynamic individually, it's time to combine them. It is possible to create colourful grooves by using different dynamic levels together in the same phrases:

Pay attention to the dynamics in the following phrases.

Example 8m:

Example 8n:

Changing dynamics through a 1/16th note roll is an excellent exercise that really helps to develop control.

Example 8o:

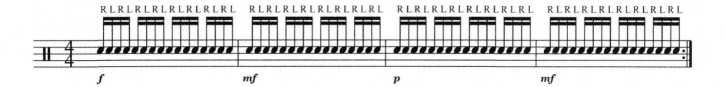

Crescendo and Decrescendo

Crescendo is a gradual increase in loudness starting from a soft dynamic level and moving to a louder one. It is indicated by the symbol '<' in notation. The opposite of crescendo, *decrescendo*, is a gradual decrease in volume from loud to soft. It is indicated by the symbol '>' in notation.

Practice crescendo and decrescendo in the following examples.

Play a two-bar crescendo from piano to forte in bars three and bar four.

Example 8p:

Play a two-bar decrescendo from forte to piano in bar three and bar four.

Example 8q:

Play a half-bar crescendo from mezzo forte to forte in bar two. Play a half-bar decrescendo from forte to mezzo forte in bar four.

Example 8r:

Play a one-bar crescendo from piano to forte in bar one. Play a one-bar decrescendo from forte to piano in bar three.

Example 8s:

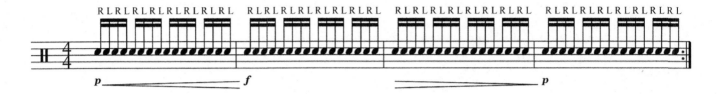

Chapter Nine

Double Bass Drum Technique

Most beginner rock drummers think that the double bass drum technique is all about speed, but this is not entirely true. Getting faster is certainly one of the main goals, but the magic word for this technique is *control*.

In this chapter, you will learn how to control your double bass drum pedals. You will also develop coordination, endurance, and balance by practicing each example. If you prefer, you can begin each example with your left foot to practice the opposite combinations.

1/8th-Note Double Bass Drum Beats

First, you will practice playing 1/8th-note double bass drum beats with 1/4-note ride patterns. As shown in the following examples, the basic foot combination of 1/8th-note beats is based on 'the 1/8th-note single-stroke roll' rudiment:

Learn the following examples and work with a metronome every day to gradually increase your speed. Start out at around 60bpm and work up to 120bpm and beyond. Keep a diary of your progress and be organised in your practice session. Practice the things you can't do, not the things you can.

At the end of every practice session, make time to *play*! Forget about practicing and have fun. If the things you were working on in the practice session come out when you play, great! If they don't, don't worry! They're just not internalised yet! It's like learning a whole new language.

Example 9a:

Example 9b:

The following examples show some 1/8th-note double bass drum variations:

Example 9c:

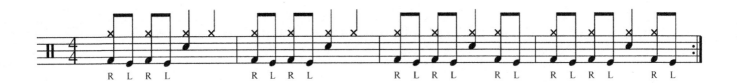

Example 9d:

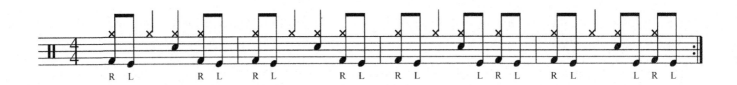

Example 9e:

Example 9f:

Example 9g:

You can also use double-stroke rolls and single paradiddles on 1/8th-note double bass drum patterns to improve your technique:

Play the 1/8th-note double-stroke roll pattern on the double bass drum.

Example 9h:

Play the 1/8th-note single paradiddle pattern on the double bass drum.

Example 9i:

1/8th-Note Triplet Double Bass Drum Beats

We can also play 1/8th-note triplets on the double bass drum. In this section we will combine them with a 1/4-note ride pattern. The following triplet double bass drum beats are based on the 1/8th-note triplet single-stroke roll rudiments you used earlier.

1/8th-note triplet single-stroke roll on the double bass drum.

Example 9j:

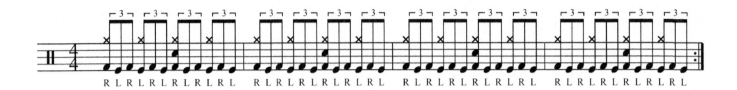

Now play this variation of the 1/8th-note triplet single-stroke roll.

Example 9k:

These triplet double bass drum variations will be a significant challenge.

Example 9l:

Example 9m:

Now try this 1/8th-note double bass drum shuffle pattern.

Example 9n:

1/16th-note Double Bass Drum Beats

1/16th-note double bass drumbeats can be combined with both with 1/4-note and 1/8th- note ride patterns. They are based on the 1/16th-note single-stroke roll rudiments you studied earlier.

The following series of examples will prepare you to play more complex grooves with double bass drumbeats.

As always, work with a metronome to gradually increase your speed once you've learnt each exercise.

Variation one: 1/16th-note single-stroke roll on the double bass drum.

Example 9o:

Variation two:

Example 9p:

Now practice the following ideas to explore new possibilities in your playing. View each exercise as starting point for your own investigations… get creative and find new ways to make these ideas musical.

Example 9q:

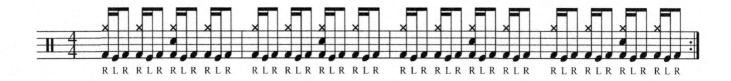

Example 9r:

R R L R R L R R L R R L   R R L R R L R R L R R L   R R L R R L R R L R R L   R R L R R L R R L R R L

Here are some examples of 1/16th-note bass drum beats with 1/8th-note ride patterns.

Here is how you play 1/16th-note single-stroke rolls on the double bass drum.

Example 9s:

R L R L R L R L R L R L R L R L   R L R L R L R L R L R L R L R L   R L R L R L R L R L R L R L R L   R L R L R L R L R L R L R L R L

Example 9t:

R L R L R L R L R L R L R L R L   R L R L R L R L R L R L R L R L   R L R L R L R L R L R L R L R L   R L R L R L R L R L R L R L R L

Example 9u:

R L R L R L R L R L R L R L R L   R L R L R L R L R L R L R L R L   R L R L R L R L R L R L R L R L   R L R L R L R L R L R L R L R L

The following variations are interesting and will challenge you in different ways.

Example 9v:

Example 9w:

Double bass drumbeats are commonly used in metal. Listen to bands such as Dream Theater, Porcupine Tree, Blind Guardian, Sepultura, Megadeath, and Metallica, and you will hear various double bass drum variations in their songs.

I recommend that you now repeat the basic groove examples from Chapters One, Two, Three, Four and Five while playing the bass drum with your weaker foot. If you complete these exercises, you will notice a quick development in your double bass drum coordination and technical ability.

Chapter Ten

2/4, 3/4, 5/4 and 7/4 Time Signatures

4/4 is the most common signature in the rock genre, but there are many different time signatures that can be used. We will study the basics of 2/4, 3/4, 5/4 and 7/4 time in this final chapter.

Playing in different time signatures will not only improve your drumming skills, it will also improve your musicality and understanding. You should always keep in mind that *counting out loud* is the key to learning in different time signatures.

The Basics of 2/4

A 2/4 time signature sounds very similar to 4/4. The main difference is that the way of counting; 2/4 is counted as *1+2+* with two-1/4 beats. Practice the following variations:

Play the 1/4-note ride pattern in 2/4.

Example 10a:

Play the 1/8th-note ride pattern in 2/4.

Example 10b:

Play the 1/16th-note ride pattern (alternating hands) in 2/4.

Example 10c:

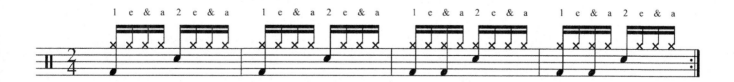

1/8th-note triplet ride pattern in 2/4.

Example 10d:

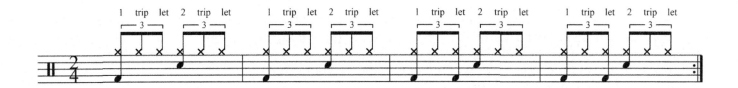

You can choose to write two triplets in 2/4-time in a 6/8 time signature. Metallica's Nothing Else Matters is a good example of a song in 6/8.

Example 10e:

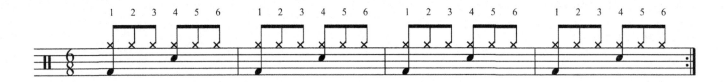

Play the 1/8th-note shuffle ride pattern in 2/4.

Example 10f:

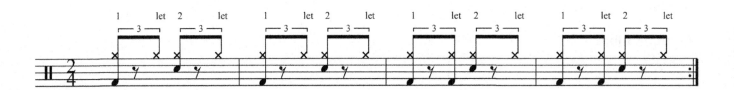

You can listen to The Who's *My Generation* (punk rock) and Three Doors Down's *Kryptonite* (alternative rock) as musical examples of 2/4-time signature.

The Basics of 3/4

A 3/4 time signature is counted as '*1+2+3+*' and contains three 1/4 beats. Practice the following examples to learn more about this time signature:

Play the 1/4-note ride pattern in 3/4.

Example 10g:

Play the 1/8th-note ride pattern in 3/4.

Example 10h:

Play the 1/16th-note ride pattern (alternating hands) in 3/4.

Example 10i:

Play the 1/8th-note triplet ride pattern in 3/4.

Example 10j:

Play the 1/8th-note shuffle ride pattern in 3/4.

Example 10k:

Neil Young's Only Love Can Break Your Heart is a good example of a song in 3/4.

Introduction to 'Odd Time Signatures'; Basics of 5/4 and 7/4 Time Signatures

Odd time signatures are meters that contain an odd number of beats (5, 7, 9, 11, 13, etc.) in each bar.

Most music you hear on the radio is in 4/4, and most people in Western society aren't used to hearing music with 5, 7, or 9 beats in the bar. There are a few exceptions, such as Pink Floyd's Money (7/4) and Seven Days by Sting (5/4), but generally, most pop music in the West is written in 4/4, 3/4, 6/8 or 12/8.

As most people aren't used to hearing them, odd time signatures can be difficult to count at first, and it is easy to become lost in the music. For this reason, musicians often combine smaller *subdivisions* to count and understand odd time signatures more easily.

Whereas 4/4 time is normally divided into two accented beats (the '2' and '4' snare hits in a backbeat), odd time signatures can be divided into various different groupings. For example, 7/4 could be counted as

1 2 3 **1** 2 **1** 2,

or

1 2 **1** 2 **1** 2 3

or

1 2 **1** 2 3 **1** 2.

A natural accent is formed on each of the '1's in the above groupings, and this has a significant effect on the music.

Count out loud, and copy the accents of the following 7/4 groupings.

First repeat the phrase, "ONE two three ONE two ONE two".

Now repeat the phrase "ONE two ONE two ONE two three".

They sound and feel very different, despite both containing seven beats.

Counting odd time signatures with smaller groups of 2 and 3 beats is called *subdivision* and how the subdivisions are organised changes how the music feels.

The Basics of 5/4

5/4 time signatures can be counted simply as '1+2+3+4+5+' but the following are also common subdivisions of the bar.

2+3: (1+2+1+2+3+).

3+2" (1+2+3+1+2+).

The series of examples below show different variations and subdivisions in 5/4.

5/4 with 2+3 subdivisions. Count and play the 1/4-note ride pattern.

Example 10l:

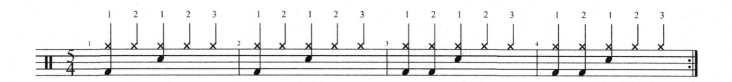

5/4 with 2+3 subdivisions. Count and play the 1/4-note ride pattern.

Example 10m:

5/4 with 2+3 subdivisions. Count and play the 1/8th-note ride pattern.

Example 10n:

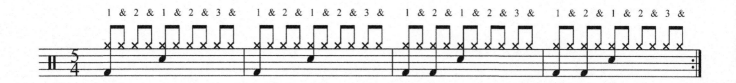

5/4 with 3+2 subdivisions. Count and play the 1/4-note ride pattern.

Example 10o:

5/4 with 3+2 subdivisions. Count and play the 1/4-note ride pattern.

Example 10p:

5/4 with 3+2 subdivisions. Count and play the 1/8th-note ride pattern.

Example 10q:

Listen to Joe Satriani's Unstoppable Momentum to hear a cool drum groove in 5/4.

The Basics of 7/4

7/4 odd time signature is counted *'1+2+3+4+5+6+7+'*

These are the most common subdivision options in 7/4:

2+2+3: '1+2+1+2+1+2+3+'.

3+2+2: '1+2+3+1+2+1+2+'

2+3+2" '1+2+1+2+3+1+2+'.

The following examples show groove variations and subdivisions in 7/4.

7/4 with 2+2+3 subdivisions. Count and play the 1/4-note ride pattern.

Example 10r:

7/4 with 2+2+3 subdivisions. Count and play the 1/4-note ride pattern.

Example 10s:

7/4 with 2+2+3 subdivisions. Count and play the 1/8th-note ride pattern.

Example 10t:

7/4 with 3+2+2 subdivisions. Count and play the 1/4-note ride pattern.

Example 10u:

7/4 with 3+2+2 subdivisions. Count and play the 1/4-note ride pattern.

Example 10v:

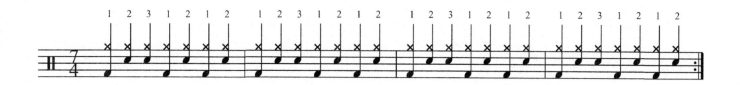

7/4 with 3+2+2 subdivisions. Count and play the 1/8th-note ride pattern.

Example 10w:

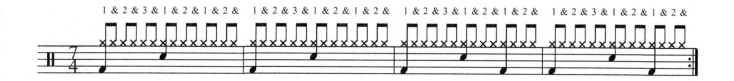

7/4 with 2+3+2 subdivisions. Count and play the 1/4-note ride pattern.

Example 10x:

7/4 with 2+3+2 subdivisions. Count and play the 1/4-note ride pattern.

Example 10y:

7/4 with 2+3+2 subdivisions. Count and play the 1/8th-note ride pattern.

Example 10z:

Pink Floyd's Money has a 7/4 and 4/4 structure. The main riff of the song is played in 7/4. It is common for progressive rock music to change the time signatures during the same song.

Conclusion

Congratulations for completing this book! Now that you have the theoretical knowledge, skills and techniques of basic rock drumming, you are ready to move on to higher levels, but it is important to maintain your skills and technique by practicing the basics regularly.

The next step is to listen to, and transcribe (figure out) the music that you want to play. This is difficult at first but one of the most beneficial skills you can learn. Continue to build on the basic skills you have learnt in this book and begin to study different genres such as jazz, Latin and funk, etc. Although these might not be your main interest right now, these genres will influence and improve your drumming skills and knowledge.

Join or form a band to gain experience and confidence in performing live music. Also, being part of a band gives you the chance to hang out with other musicians, play songs you like, and, most importantly, enjoy your time as a drummer.

Thank you once again for reading and working through this book. I wish you all the best in your musical journey!

"Drumming is not worrying about what you can't do, it is about having fun with what you can do." – Chris Adler.

Rock on...

Serkan Süer

About the Author:

Serkan Süer was born in Turkey, 1979 and is currently living in Halifax, Canada. He has been playing drums for 23 years. He has been performing as a session musician for and playing as a stage musician for different projects in various musical styles. His band Soul Project released their album Out of The Circle in 2010. His band Tayfa released their album Rahat in 2015.

Serkan has been teaching drums professionally for 15 years and completed the Berklee College of Music Specialist Drummer Certificate in 2014 after being tutored by Rod Morgenstein, Jim Payne, and Yoron Israel. He completed a Master's Degree in Adult Education at Ankara University in 2011.

Acknowledgements:

This book is dedicated to my wonderful parents, my wife and my daughter. I thank them for their unconditional support. I also want to thank Fundamental Changes, my instructors Rod Morgenstein, Jim Payne and Yoron Israel from Berklee, the talented musicians and producers I have worked with, all my students and my precious friends.

Other Drum Books from Fundamental Changes

50 Essential Warmups for Drums

Rhythm and Notation for Drums

Other Guitar Books from Fundamental Changes

The Complete Guide to Playing Blues Guitar Book One: Rhythm Guitar

The Complete Guide to Playing Blues Guitar Book Two: Melodic Phrasing

The Complete Guide to Playing Blues Guitar Book Three: Beyond Pentatonics

The Complete Guide to Playing Blues Guitar Compilation

The CAGED System and 100 Licks for Blues Guitar

Fundamental Changes in Jazz Guitar: The Major ii V I

Minor ii V Mastery for Jazz Guitar

Jazz Blues Soloing for Guitar

Guitar Scales in Context

Guitar Chords in Context

The First 100 Chords for Guitar

Jazz Guitar Chord Mastery

Complete Technique for Modern Guitar

Funk Guitar Mastery

The Complete Technique, Theory and Scales Compilation for Guitar

Sight Reading Mastery for Guitar

Rock Guitar Un-CAGED: The CAGED System and 100 Licks for Rock Guitar

The Practical Guide to Modern Music Theory for Guitarists

Beginner's Guitar Lessons: The Essential Guide

Chord Tone Soloing for Jazz Guitar

Heavy Metal Rhythm Guitar

Heavy Metal Lead Guitar

Progressive Metal Guitar

Heavy Metal Guitar Bible

Exotic Pentatonic Soloing for Guitar

Voice Leading Jazz Guitar

The Complete Jazz Soloing Compilation

The Jazz Guitar Chords Compilation

Fingerstyle Blues Guitar

The Complete DADGAD Guitar Method

Country Guitar for Beginners

Beginner Lead Guitar Method

Printed in Great Britain
by Amazon